DISCARD

Fact Finders®

CAUSE AND EFFECT: AMERICAN INDIAN HISTORY

Last Battle

CAUSES AND EFFECTS of the Massacre at Wounded Knee

BY PAMELA DELL

Consultant:
Brett Barker, PhD
Associate Professor of History
University of Wisconsin–Marathon County

CAPSTONE PRESS
a capstone imprint

Fact Finders Books are published by Capstone Press,
1710 Roe Crest Drive, North Mankato, Minnesota 56003
www.capstonepub.com

Library of Congress Cataloging-in-Publication Data
Dell, Pamela.
 Last battle : causes and effects of the Massacre at Wounded Knee / By Pamela Dell.
  pages cm.—(Fact finders. Cause and effect: American Indian history)
 Includes bibliographical references and index.
 Summary: "Explains the massacre at Wounded Knee in 1890, including its chronology, causes, and lasting effects"—Provided by publisher.
 ISBN 978-1-4914-4835-9 (library binding)
 ISBN 978-1-4914-4903-5 (paperback)
 ISBN 978-1-4914-4921-9 (ebook pdf)
1. Wounded Knee Massacre, S.D., 1890—Juvenile literature. I. Title.
 E83.89.D45 2016
 973.8'6—dc23   2015010000

Editorial Credits
Catherine Neitge, editor and designer; Bobbie Nuytten, designer;
Eric Gohl, media researcher; Karina Rose, production specialist

Source Notes
Page 21, line 1:"Dakota Doctor Witnesses Wounded Knee Aftermath." Native Voices. U.S. National Library of Medicine. 16 April 2015. http://www.nlm.nih.gov/nativevoices/timeline/378.html?tribe=Dakota
Page 27, line 12: "On Wounded Knee." *The New York Times*. 23 Oct. 2012. 16 April 2015. http://www.nytimes.com/2012/10/24/opinion/the-siege-of-wounded-knee.html

Photo Credits
Alamy: Allen Russell, 28; Capstone: 18; Corbis: Bettmann, 21, 26; Courtesy of Peter A. Campbell: cover; CriaImages.com: Jay Robert Nash Collection, 11, 12; Granger, NYC: 13, 14, 25; Library of Congress: 9, 19, 23; National Archives and Records Administration: 16; Newscom: akg-images, 7, 17, G. E. Trager Picture History, 15, ZUMA Press/Kevin McKiernan, 27; SuperStock: 5; Wikimedia: Public Domain, 20

Design Elements: Shutterstock

Printed in Canada.

052015   008825FRF15

FEBRUARY 2016

Table of Contents

CULTURES CLASH

Long before Europeans arrived in North America, the American Indians of the Great Sioux Nation roamed the **Great Plains**. The largest group in the Sioux nation, the Lakota, lived mainly in North and South Dakota. Their homelands included South Dakota's Black Hills, an area **sacred** to them.

As early as 1825, the U.S. government recognized the Lakota's rights to their homelands. But white people wanted the land. As more of them came west, things began to change. Whites and Lakota clashed, often violently.

The government created the **Treaty** of Fort Laramie in 1868 to deal with these troubles. The agreement promised the Lakota their land forever. Whites were not to settle there. In exchange, the Lakota would allow settlers to pass through unharmed.

But 22 years later, great harm came to that land. Few whites suffered, however. The victims were the Lakota, killed at a place called Wounded Knee Creek.

The Lakota relied on the buffalo for food, clothing, tepees, tools, and more.

FAST FACT

The Dakota and Nakota are also part of the Great Sioux Nation. The Lakota are the largest group.

Great Plains—the broad, level land that stretches eastward from the base of the Rocky Mountains for about 400 miles (644 kilometers) in the United States and Canada
sacred—holy
treaty—an official agreement between two or more groups or countries

What Caused the MASSACRE AT WOUNDED KNEE?

Like other American Indians across the nation in the 1800s, the Sioux fought courageously to protect their homelands. The Wounded Knee **Massacre**, a tragic moment in the struggle by the Lakota, had many causes.

Cause #1: Stolen Lands

The U.S. government had set up the Great Sioux **Reservation** under the 1868 Treaty of Fort Laramie. The vast territory, including the Black Hills, belonged only to the Sioux. But whites refused to respect the legal territorial boundaries.

Army Lieutenant Colonel George Custer and his 7th Cavalry came to South Dakota to explore the Black Hills in 1874. When they discovered gold, white settlers rushed to grab the land. The government looked the other way, ignoring Lakota rights.

massacre—the deliberate killing of a group of unarmed people
reservation—area of land set aside by the U.S. government for American Indians; in Canada reservations are called reserves
hostiles—historically, soldiers' term for unfriendly American Indians

The following year U.S. President Ulysses S. Grant offered the Lakota $6 million to purchase the Black Hills. The Lakota refused. The government then ordered all Sioux not already living on their reservation to relocate there. Any who did not comply would be considered "**hostiles**" and rounded up by the army. The treaty said the Lakota had the right to hunt buffalo outside the reservation. So to the Lakota, Grant's order was a declaration of war.

The Battle of the Little Bighorn

George Custer was killed by the Lakota and their Cheyenne allies in one of history's most well-known battles. Custer and his 7th Cavalry faced Lakota chief Sitting Bull and his warriors. The Battle of the Little Bighorn in Montana took place June 25–26, 1876. To the shock of white Americans, Custer was defeated and killed, along with more than 200 of his men.

The United States' response to the stunning defeat was total war against the Sioux. The army starved the Lakota by killing their main food source, the buffalo. Soldiers destroyed Lakota camps. Within a year most Lakota were on the reservation, which was much reduced in size. The government seized the Black Hills, in direct violation of the Treaty of Fort Laramie.

Artist Charles Russell's 1903 painting depicts the defeat of Custer and his men at the Battle of the Little Bighorn.

Cause #2: The Dawes Act

The U.S. Congress passed the Dawes Act in 1887. Also known as the General **Allotment** Act, it offered parcels of reservation land to individual American Indians. The government hoped the Indians would take up farming. This was part of its plan to "Americanize" the Lakota and other Indians.

The law failed miserably. Like many Indians, the Lakota rebelled, not wanting to settle down and farm. They wanted to keep their lifestyle of roaming and hunting. In addition, much of the land was not suitable for farming.

The Great Sioux Reservation set up in 1868 had comprised all of present-day South Dakota west of the Missouri River. Two years after passage of the Dawes Act, Congress broke it into smaller reservations.

allotment—specific amount of something given to a person or group

Swiss artist Karl Bodmer painted a watercolor of a Sioux camp in 1833.

Battle Over the Black Hills

By breaking the Treaty of Fort Laramie, the U.S. wrongfully took the Black Hills from the Lakota. In 1980 the U.S. Supreme Court ordered the government to pay for the land it took 100 years earlier.

After the ruling the government offered the Lakota more than $100 million. As before, they refused. The money was set aside and, with interest, now totals more than $1 billion. By not accepting the money, the Lakota are making a point. Their sacred lands are rightfully theirs—and not for sale.

Cause #3: The Ghost Dance

The Lakota's world was being destroyed. In 1889, increasingly desperate, many began practicing the Ghost Dance religion. Its leader, a Paiute Indian named Wovoka, advised hard work and nonviolence toward whites. Wovoka said the religion's followers would be reunited with dead relatives and white people would disappear. He said buffalo would again fill the plains.

Wovoka was also known as Jack Wilson.

The Ghost Dance ceremony was long and tiring. The dancing continued for five days. After eating blessed food, the believers joined hands and danced in a circle. Their singing rose from a slow, quiet tempo to become increasingly loud and fast. Men, women, and children all joined in. People often fell into trances, hoping to meet dead loved ones.

The Ghost Dance caught on quickly. But the wild dancing made whites suspicious. The government feared the Lakota were working up to a great rebellion.

For the beaten-down, robbed, and starving Lakota, becoming believers was a last grasp for hope. For the whites, however, this strange dance was the last straw.

The Bitter
ROAD TO DEATH

Some Lakota agreed with Wovoka that acting peacefully would help them. Others wanted to overthrow the whites. The Ghost Dance helped the **militants** encourage this idea. Many warriors started wearing "ghost shirts." They believed the white shirts protected them from gunfire.

Some ghost shirts were plain. Others were decorated with feathers, fringe, and painted symbols.

14

An Oglala band was camped at Pine Ridge one month before the massacre at Wounded Knee.

In late 1889 white settlers began demanding military protection. Agents who ran the Pine Ridge and Rosebud Indian reservations believed the dance threatened their control. When troops armed with guns and cannons were called to the reservations, tensions exploded. Many Ghost Dancers fled to a far corner of Pine Ridge.

militant—person who supports extreme action in pursuing a cause

Closing in on the Chiefs

As fear increased on both sides, Army General Nelson A. Miles ordered the arrest of two Lakota chiefs in November 1890. His targets were Hunkpapa Lakota chief Sitting Bull and Big Foot, a Miniconjou Lakota chief.

Miles, the officer in charge, considered both to be hostiles. He felt they were pushing their people toward war.

Sitting Bull was shot and killed by reservation police when they attempted to arrest him December 15. His 17-year-old son also died.

Sitting Bull was a fearless chief and spiritual leader.

On December 28, after searching unsuccessfully, Miles' troops finally caught up with Big Foot and about 350 followers. They had been trying to reach the safety of Pine Ridge. Big Foot was seriously ill with pneumonia. The Lakota surrendered willingly and were marched to Wounded Knee Creek to make camp.

Big Foot's Lakota name was Si Tanka, Spotted Elk. He was a skilled peacemaker.

Trouble Erupts

Big Foot and his followers found themselves surrounded by tense, armed troops on the morning of December 29, 1890. The men were from the 7th Cavalry, formerly Custer's regiment. The 500 soldiers had rifles and heavier weapons.

The Lakota had not resisted capture. They were freezing, starving, angry, and afraid. But when the military commander ordered the warriors to turn over their weapons, tempers flared. A deaf Lakota named Black Coyote began scuffling with a soldier trying to take his rifle. He had not heard the order to give up his weapon. The gun fired.

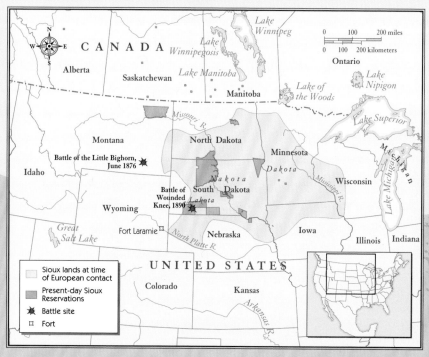

The Great Sioux Reservation was broken into smaller reservations and did not include the Black Hills.

Troops as close as 10 feet (3 meters) to the warriors immediately started shooting. About half the Lakota men died instantly. Those still alive tried to fight back with any weapons they had, including tomahawks and knives. Overpowered and outnumbered, they turned and fled with their families. The soldiers followed them on horseback. Finally, the soldiers aimed their cannons at Lakota hiding in a ravine and continued blasting away. Some believed the extreme violence was the 7th Cavalry's way of getting back at the Lakota for the Little Bighorn defeat.

Members of the 7th Cavalry posed with their cannons, known as Hotchkiss guns, after the massacre.

Counting the Dead

Wounded Knee was the scene of a gruesome massacre. Afterward, troops carried some dead and wounded away. But a raging winter storm soon stopped the search for bodies.

The search did not resume until January 3, 1891. The Pine Ridge doctor, Charles Eastman, a Santee Dakota, came back to Wounded Knee with the soldiers. What he reported was shocking. Chief Big Foot lay dead and frozen in the snow, along with scores of Lakota. Some dead lay as far away as 3 miles (4.8 km), where soldiers had gunned them down.

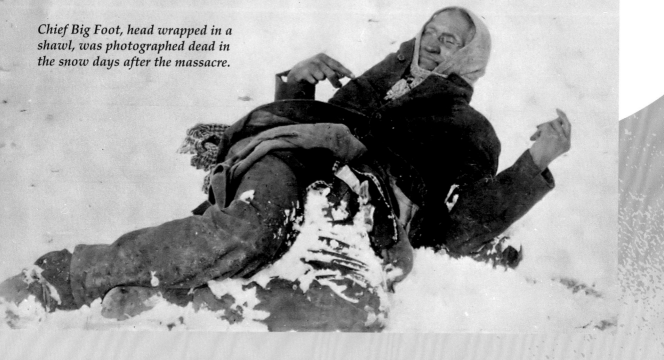

Chief Big Foot, head wrapped in a shawl, was photographed dead in the snow days after the massacre.

Among the dead bodies, Dr. Charles Eastman found a baby girl who had survived. She was adopted by an Army officer.

Soldiers returned to the massacre site to bury victims in a mass grave.

Eastman later wrote, "[W]e found them scattered along as they had been relentlessly hunted down and slaughtered, while fleeing for their lives."

The soldiers recovered the bodies of 84 men and boys, 44 women, and 18 children. They buried the dead in a mass grave.

The number of Lakota dead is not known. But some historians believe it was probably about 300, mostly women and children. The army lost 25 men. Most of them were accidentally shot by other U.S. soldiers during the fighting.

What Effects Did the MASSACRE AT WOUNDED KNEE HAVE?

The one-sided assault at Wounded Knee Creek ended a way of life for the Lakota. The effects of the massacre ripple through time even until today.

Effect #1: Loss of a Way of Life

The massacre at Wounded Knee is considered the last conflict of the Indian wars. Many Lakota who survived the massacre fled to distant parts of their tribal lands. Some continued to furiously practice the Ghost Dance. Soon, however, the Lakota were forced back to Pine Ridge and other reservations.

After the massacre the Lakota continued to experience an attempt by whites to destroy their culture. Their Ghost Dance religion was outlawed. Anyone found practicing it could be hanged. Lakota systems of government were shut down. Their children were forced to attend boarding schools whose purpose was to "civilize" them. The children, taught that their culture was bad, were forbidden to speak their own language.

The threats to their culture, land, and way of living brought widespread despair among the Lakota and other American Indians. Life on the reservations often meant extreme poverty, poor education, and alcoholism. The harshness of this life did not kill off Lakota pride, however. Family ties remained strong and cultural traditions did not die.

Book Tells of Loss

Bury My Heart at Wounded Knee: An Indian History of the American West by Dee Brown was published in 1970. The highly acclaimed book details the horrible losses of American Indians who were robbed of their lands and property and forced onto reservations. It was one of the first history books to give the American Indians' point of view. It has sold millions of copies and is still popular today.

When the photo was taken in 1891, the original caption read "What's left of Big Foot's Band. Taken near Deadwood, South Dakota in 1891."

Effect #2: Questionable Honor

Wounded Knee was not a battle in any realistic sense. It was a massacre. General Miles agreed and blamed Colonel James Forsyth, commander that day. Miles relieved Forsyth of his command and said he had deliberately disobeyed his orders. But in early 1891, an investigation found Forsyth not guilty of any wrongdoing. He was reinstated as commander of the 7th Cavalry.

Further, for their roles in the murderous attack, 20 soldiers received Medals of Honor. It is the highest medal the military awards.

The U.S. Congress finally apologized to the descendants of those killed or hurt at Wounded Knee. The House and Senate in 1990 approved a resolution expressing the government's "deep regret" for the massacre on the Pine Ridge Indian Reservation 100 years earlier.

The Lakota and others continue to fight to have the Medals of Honor overturned, calling them medals of dishonor. A **petition** started in 2013 requests that President Obama take action.

Newspaper coverage immediately following the massacre at Wounded Knee referred to the "heroic" 7th Cavalry.

petition—letter signed by many people asking leaders for a change

Effect #3: Return to Wounded Knee

Two hundred Lakota and other Indians staged a powerful protest on February 27, 1973. American Indian Movement (AIM) protesters took over the town of Wounded Knee on the Pine Ridge Reservation. They chose the site for its strong symbolism. The **siege** lasted 71 days. Tensions ran high but the plight of the Lakota and all Indians got widespread attention.

The AIM protesters were calling attention to terrible reservation living conditions, long-standing treaty violations, and what they saw as corrupt tribal government.

Government agents looked down upon the church at Wounded Knee where protesters gathered during the standoff.

siege—an attack designed to surround a place and cut it off from supplies or help

acquitted—declared not guilty of a crime

During the takeover government agents fired thousands of rounds of ammunition at the protesters, who returned fire. Two Indians were killed and 12 people were wounded, including two government agents. After the protesters surrendered, more than 1,200 people were arrested and charged with various crimes. Almost all were later **acquitted**.

"There were other actions and protests," said Paul Chaat Smith, who works at the National Museum of the American Indian. "But none came close to capturing the imagination of the Indian world or challenging American power."

AIM leader Dennis Banks, who played a leading role in the takeover, said it changed Indians' attitudes for the better.

FAST FACT

AIM formed in 1968 in Minneapolis, Minnesota, to help urban Indians who faced racism, unemployment, and lack of decent housing. AIM members also fight for treaty rights and the return of tribal lands.

The annual memorial ride begins in mid-December.

Memorial Ride

Every December a group of Lakota honor those who died at Wounded Knee with a memorial horseback ride. It was first organized in 1986 as the Chief Big Foot Memorial Ride. Today the two-week ride of nearly 300 miles (483 km) is called the Oomaka Tokatakiya (Future Generations) ride. Its organizers say it honors the past while fostering leadership qualities in the young Lakota riders.

The ride starts near Bullhead, South Dakota, where Sitting Bull was killed, and traces the route some of his followers took to reach his fellow chief, Big Foot. The ride continues to Wounded Knee where hundreds were killed.

TIMELINE

1825:
A treaty with the U.S. government confirms Sioux possession of lands ranging from Wisconsin to Wyoming.

1868:
The Treaty of Fort Laramie establishes the Great Sioux Reservation and promises to protect the sacred Black Hills and other Lakota lands from white invasion.

1874:
Lieutenant Colonel George A. Custer leads an expedition into the Black Hills, where gold is discovered.

1875:
The U.S. government offers the Lakota $6 million for rights to the Black Hills. The Lakota refuse.

June 25-26, 1876:
Lakota chief Sitting Bull leads Lakota and Cheyenne warriors to victory at the Battle of the Little Bighorn.

1887:
Congress passes the General Allotment Act, also known as the Dawes Act.

1889:
As a desperate last hope, the Lakota begin practicing the Ghost Dance religion.

November 1890:
General Nelson A. Miles orders the arrest of Lakota chiefs Sitting Bull and Big Foot.

December 15, 1890:
Police shoot and kill Sitting Bull while trying to arrest him.

December 28, 1890:
Army troops catch up with Big Foot and about 350 of his followers. They are marched to a campsite at Wounded Knee Creek.

December 29, 1890:
After a Lakota's gun goes off, Army troops launch into a slaughter of the Lakota camped at Wounded Knee Creek.

January 3, 1891:
U.S. soldiers return to Wounded Knee Creek with a burial party to search for Lakota dead and wounded.

1891:
An investigation finds Colonel James Forsyth blameless of any wrongdoing at Wounded Knee. Twenty soldiers receive the military's highest award, the Medal of Honor, for their roles in the attack.

February 27, 1973:
American Indian Movement protesters and their supporters take over the town of Wounded Knee, starting a 71-day occupation. Most of the 1,200 people arrested and charged with crimes were acquitted.

1980:
The U.S. Supreme Court orders the government to pay the Great Sioux Nation $102 million as compensation for taking the Black Hills. The Sioux refuse to accept the offer, which is now worth more than $1 billion.

1990:
Congress apologizes to the descendants of those killed or wounded at the Wounded Knee massacre.

2013:
A petition begins circulating requesting President Obama to take away the Medals of Honor awarded in 1891.

GLOSSARY

acquitted (uh-KWIT-ted)—declared not guilty of a crime

allotment (uh-LOT-ment)—specific amount of something given to a person or group

Great Plains (GRAYT PLANES)—the broad, level land that stretches eastward from the base of the Rocky Mountains for about 400 miles (644 km) in the United States and Canada

hostiles (HOSS-tuhls)—historically, soldiers' term for unfriendly American Indians

massacre (MASS-uh-kuhr)—the deliberate killing of a group of unarmed people

militant (MIL-uh-tuhnt)—person who supports extreme action in pursuing a cause

petition (ree-uh-NAKT)—letter signed by many people asking leaders for a change

reservation (rez-er-VAY-shuhn)—area of land set aside by the U.S. government for American Indians; in Canada reservations are called reserves

sacred (SAY-krid)—holy

siege (SEEJ)—an attack designed to surround a place and cut it off from supplies or help

treaty (TREE-tee)—an official agreement between two or more groups or countries

READ MORE

Collins, Terry. *Into the West: Causes and Effects of U.S. Westward Expansion*. North Mankato, Minn.: Capstone, 2014.

Higgins, Nadia. *Defending the Land: Causes and Effects of Red Cloud's War*. North Mankato, Minn.: Capstone, 2015.

Stanley, George E. *Sitting Bull: Great Sioux Hero*. New York: Sterling, 2010.

Zimmerman, Dwight Jon. *Saga of the Sioux: An Adaptation from Dee Brown's Bury My Heart at Wounded Knee*. New York: Henry Holt, 2011.

INTERNET SITES

FactHound offers a safe, fun way to find Internet sites related to this book. All of the sites on FactHound have been researched by our staff.

Here's all you do:

Visit *www.facthound.com*

Type in this code: 9781491448359

Super-cool stuff!

Check out projects, games and lots more at
www.capstonekids.com

CRITICAL THINKING USING THE COMMON CORE

1. Why did the U.S. government break the 1868 Treaty of Fort Laramie? What did the Americans want? (Key Ideas and Details)

2. Explain the Ghost Dance ritual and name three things the dance was supposed to accomplish for the Lakota. (Key Ideas and Details)

3. Examine the map on page 18. What states were part of the original Sioux homeland? In what states are Sioux reservations today? (Craft and Structure)

INDEX